How To Invest In Real Estate If You have No Money

How to Invest in Real Estate While Working a Full-Time Job

Charles John

All rights reserved. No part of this publication may be reproduced, distributed, or transmitted in any form or by any means, including photocopying, recording or other electronic or mechanical methods, without the prior written permission of the publisher, except in the case of brief quotations embodied in critical reviews and certain other noncommercial uses permitted by copyright law.

Copyright © Charles John, 2023.

Table of contents

CHAPTER ONE

How to Make Real Estate Investments Without Money

Can A Person With A Poor Credit Purchase Real estate?

CHAPTER TWO

How to Invest in Real Estate While Working a Full-Time Job

Real estate investing while maintaining a full-time career offers several benefits

CHAPTER THREE

Investing in Real Estate for Dummies

Real Estate Mutual Funds

Why Make a Real Estate Investment?

REITs vs. landlords: Benefits And Drawbacks

How Do You Invest In Real Estate?

How Can Investing in Real Estate Be Successful?

Tips For Beginners On Real Estate Investing

Real Estate Investment Groups (REIG)

INVESTING IN PROPERTY FOR NEWCOMERS

Mistakes To Avoid When Investing In Real Estate

Real Estate Terminology Newcomers Need to Know

CHAPTER FOUR

What Sets Limited Liability Companies Apart From Corporations?

Differences between an LLC and a corporation

The Crucial Difference Between a Tax Entity and a Legal Entity

Corporations and LLCs and their Tax Effects

REAL ESTATE INVESTMENT STRATEGY

CHAPTER ONE

Successful real estate investors have the ability to understand, recognize, and profit from other people's money. This is what makes them successful. Why? because they are experts at investing in real estate without using their own money. For newer and less wealthy investors who lack the appropriate funds or credit, this is an alluring way to break into the real estate market. On the other side, seasoned investors have found that using other people's money allows them to sell their available funds, freeing up their capital to invest more and ultimately generate more money.

If you want to learn how to invest in real estate without having any of your own money, you're in luck. You don't necessarily need to invest money in it to get started, at the very least. If you do not want to use your own money to invest, you will also need a trustworthy network. The problem is figuring out who can help you and how to work with them.

There is no doubt that investing in real estate without using any of your own funds is possible. To purchase a deal, you don't need to have an endless quantity of cash on hand. You must be knowledgeable about real estate investing and have the right people on your side. If you'd like to put money into real estate with no money of your own, may I refer you to the following?

How to Make Real Estate Investments Without Money

The real estate market sees a significant amount of investment transactions every year. While most of them are finished using traditional lenders and institutions, such banks, some of them are finished utilizing less traditional techniques. The investor's inability to raise the required finances or lack of the required credit score is often the cause of this. Here are 11 suggestions for investing in real estate without any money:

*Lenders of payday loans

*Private capital lenders

*Wholesaling

Investment Joint Ventures

Mortgage Equity

*Application Option

Consumer Financing

*Residence hacking

government loans

*Microloans

*REITs

While there are many benefits to investing in real estate with no money down, it's important to keep in mind that not all cashless transactions are worthwhile. Aside from having additional working capital options available to them, investors with high credit scores will also have more control over their financial commitments. It is in your best advantage to maintain that score at a high level in order to save the most money as a real estate investor.

However, there are other situations where making these decisions makes more sense. Take into account the fact that cash purchasers are perceived as more direct than loan purchases compared to conventional loans, which require more time to execute. If you have cash on hand, this strategy can provide you a unique advantage at the negotiation table.

Investors should be aware that there are still options available to them if they lack the cash or credit necessary to purchase a home conventionally. You can invest in real estate without using any of your own money if you comprehend the many strategies described below:

1. Hard cash king

In contrast to private loans, hard money lenders charge fees in the form of points. These points, which can range from three to five, denote an additional upfront percentage fee based on the borrowed amount in addition to the interest rates hard money lenders charge, which range between 10 and 18 percent. Investors should do their homework because hard/private money lenders don't always have the same fees and interest rates.

2. Particular Lenders

Investors frequently pay between 6 and 12 percent interest on private money loans, which speed up and streamline every transaction. The most popular method for financing no money down real estate projects is to use hard or private money lenders. These loans aren't given out by banks, but rather by individuals and businesses seeking to fund profitable investments. These loans generally have additional restrictions of their own, such as additional fees and higher interest rates. When employing these types of lenders, a good general rule of thumb is to look for homes that may be purchased for 50 cents on the dollar.

3. Wholesale

A high credit score or a significant down payment are not prerequisites for the wholesaling method of real estate investing. Instead, having the appropriate numbers in place is all that is necessary. Finding inexpensive properties, handing over the contract to a prospective buyer, and receiving payment are the three main components of real estate wholesaling.

4. Equity-based joint ventures
Partnerships for investing in real estate are pretty typical. According to Edward Shaw, a co-founder of Leeline Sourcing, forming partnerships is a common real estate investing strategy. Your weaknesses as an investor can be compensated for by someone else. In many partnerships, one partner will purchase an undervalued distressed property, while the other will finance it using their creditworthiness and available finances.

5. Home Equity

Another option for investors without a down payment is home equity. This is a possible option because recent increases in home values may make more money available than you think. Investors can often take advantage of this technique in one of two ways: either by rewriting the original loan and carrying out a cash-out refinance, or by leaving the original loan in place and adding a home equity line of credit.

6. Option to Buy

Investors can buy buildings using this method, sometimes known as a "lease-option," without instantly becoming owners. However, the investor will formally consent to buy the house from the owner in the future at a specific price. In return, the investor agrees to lease the home for a longer length of time.

7. Buyer Financing

In contrast to traditional loans, seller financing works as follows: instead of going through a bank, the investor purchases the home directly from the homeowner/seller, and the two parties sign a contract describing the agreed-upon interest rate, payback schedule, and default penalties.

8. Home invasion

House hacking, as the name suggests, is a real estate strategy that enables savvy investors to profit from a unique situation. But with this particular exit strategy, investors will make money by renting out their primary residence. Owners of multi-unit homes, for example, may choose to rent out the areas they don't use. In this strategy, the rent money could potentially be utilized to settle the owner's mortgage. However, those who are alive in single-family homes could decide to rent bedrooms when they can. In either case, home hacking enables investors to reduce the risk of vacancy while simultaneously increasing cash flow.

9. Federal loans

Government loans could be the best-known financial option available to investors right now. Below is a list of government loans that you may already be familiar with:

FHA financing

USDA Loan

The VA Loan

"Good Neighbor Next Door" program

Fannie Mae or Freddie Mac?

Energy-Efficient Mortgage (EEM)

FHA Rule *203 (k)

To Native Americans: *Loan

Local Programs & Grants

It is crucial to keep in mind that there are some aspects of government loans that make them unsuitable for making quick money on home improvements. For example, a VA Loan may only be used to finance one property. However, compared to hard money and private lenders, FHA loans usually have substantially longer loan periods. Additionally, almost all government loans can take months to receive approval, making them less attractive than just about every other option on this list.

If you use a USDA or VA loan, especially if you initially purchase your potential rental properties as your home, you may have access to more flexible options. This is mainly useful when attempting to invest in real estate with little or no money. You can purchase a home with no money down as long as you plan to live there for at least a year as your primary residence before renting it out after you move out. Both your primary property and your rented properties count toward equity building. Credit score and down payment requirements are also more forgiving when purchasing a main residence. Living in residences that you plan to rent out is a common tactic to get past more stringent loan restrictions.

FHA loans only need a 3.5% down payment for duplex financing if you live in one apartment. The second half of your duplex can then be rented out for more money. For those who are just starting to put a little of their own money into real estate, this strategy can be useful. With a little down payment and an increase in rent, you may pay off a sizable portion of your mortgage payments.

10. Microfinance

As the peer-to-peer economy continues to have an impact on how real estate investors conduct business, microloans will remain an option. Anyone can invest in real estate thanks to microloans, a sort of peer-to-peer lending where the lenders are ordinary individuals rather than banks and credit unions. Microloans can be issued by a single lender or aggregated across several investors, each of whom is expected to contribute a portion of the borrower's

11. Purchasing REITs

Real estate investment trusts, or REITs, are an excellent location to start investing in real estate. Instead of purchasing physical properties, investors purchase stock in a company that develops or maintains real estate. This is how purchasing REITs is comparable to purchasing stocks, however REITS still allow investors to benefit from all that real estate has to offer. Through REITs, you may invest in real estate and generate passive income without having to make any of your own investments.

how to make real estate investments on a budget

Can A Person With A Poor Credit Purchase Real estate?

no credit or money? No problem. For newbies looking for advice on how to invest in real estate with no money down and low credit, understanding your credit score is the first step. This figure, which is essentially a statistical instrument used by lenders to determine the likelihood that you would repay the money you borrowed, is essential when securing financing for real estate. Higher quality scores result in better mortgage rates, which in turn translate into long-term savings that ultimately benefit you, the investor.

Credit ratings are almost usually based on scoring models, with FICO being the most popular model. These scores eventually define a person's creditworthiness, which range from 300 to 850. It resembles this in some ways:

*300–600 for those with poor credit

*600 to 649 if you have terrible credit

*For Fair Credit, 650 to 699

*Outstanding Credit: 700-749

*750-850 Outstanding Credit

Although each credit agency will have its own evaluation systems that are based on different aspects, the most common credit score calculations are based on five basic elements.

-Payment History is valued at 35%.

-30% of outstanding balances

-15% for the length of credit history

-10% of all Account Types

Credit inquiry volume is 10%. The first step is to understand how your credit score impacts your future investing plan and to be aware of it. Depending on your credit score, you might be eligible for a conventional loan and for down payment assistance. Your strategies for investing in real estate and your financing options will both benefit from knowing where you stand financially in terms of credit. Although understanding how to invest with no money down is essential for investors, this approach isn't always the ideal one.

Stopping Homelessness

A phrase used in banking and real estate is "house-poor." The expression describes people who overextend themselves when buying a home and run out of money for unexpected expenses. These households are in such a precarious financial position that it is difficult to recover when unforeseen events like a job loss or broken equipment occur. Unfortunately, this is all too frequent when attempting to invest in real estate without any money.

There are a few steps you may take when purchasing real estate to avoid financial problems. Always keep your emergency money separate from other funds and don't include it in your budget projections while buying a home. You would always have money to fall back on in such a situation. In certain cases, conserving your emergency cash may force you to make a smaller down payment than you would like. Remember that even if you initially need mortgage insurance, you can refinance at a later time when you have more equity in the home.

Summary

Do you understand how to invest in real estate without using any of your own funds? Even if your credit score is low, you can start investing right away using a number of strategies. Consider your options if you want to start a new career and better your financial situation. Do you want to take any additional chances now that you know you can? Now that you are aware that it is possible to own property without using any of your own money, what will you do?

CHAPTER TWO

How to Invest in Real Estate While Working a Full-Time Job

Your full-time employment now hinders you from investing in real estate, despite your desire to do so. Currently, resigning is not a financially viable option, and keeping your 9 to 5 job while investing may have benefits. Your ambition to invest in real estate should be supported by your job rather than hindered by it.

Real estate investing while maintaining a full-time career offers several benefits:

*Your revenue will support your investments.

*A simpler application process for bank loans

*At work, chances to network professionally are constantly available.

*Options for Investing While Working Full-Time

* Create a website

Spend money while you sleep. A website is an excellent instrument for promoting and legitimizing your brand-new business ventures. Include information and clear, expert images to entice potential tenants of your home. Include a quick and simple manner for people to get in touch with you as well.

*Utilize a virtual assistant.

If you can afford their services, a virtual assistant might be invaluable. Send them emails often so you can accomplish things while you're at work. Give them access to the phone while you're away and ask them to handle the everyday administrative jobs you don't have time to perform. You are always accessible when you operate as a virtual assistant, even during regular business hours.

*Collaborate with the property manager

It could seem like an extra expense to hire a property manager. Isn't owning and managing your own properties one of the goals of investing? But suppose that while you are in a meeting, one of your tenants is bothering you about a leak, or your home is empty and you don't have time to find a tenant. This indicates that you are losing more cash than you would be paying a management firm. Let them handle the problems that could cost you a lot of money.

*Be a partner in a limited partnership with reputable investors.

No one is forcing you to go it alone. The expense and responsibilities can occasionally be reduced by 50% by finding a partner investor. However, don't rush into this decision. You don't want a relationship to end in divorce because it's similar to a marriage. You can work a full-time job and pursue your passion to invest in real estate part-time. With effective time management strategies, a task-oriented mindset, and some help, you might be able to realize your vision.

CHAPTER THREE

Investing in Real Estate for Dummies

When you think of investing in real estate, your house typically comes to mind first.

Naturally, real estate investors have a wide range of options when it comes to investing, so they don't always involve actual buildings. Real estate has become more well-liked as an investment over the past 50 years or more. The greatest possibilities for individual investors are listed below, along with some justifications for doing so.

KEY LESSONS

Real estate, which is viewed as a distinct asset class, should at the very least be included in a well-diversified portfolio. One of the finest ways for investors to make money is through real estate investment and landlording. Flippers look to buy undervalued real estate, fix it up, and resell it for a profit. Real estate investment trusts (REITs) provide indirect real estate exposure without the need to own, manage, or finance real estate.

Historical Prices

Real estate has long been viewed as a prudent investment, and for good reason. Historical housing statistics before 2007 provided the idea that prices would continue to climb indefinitely. The average sale price of homes in the United States increased every year, with few exceptions, between 1963 and 2007, which marked the start of the Great Recession. There was a modest fall in housing values at the beginning of the COVID-19 outbreak in the spring of 2020. However, as vaccines were introduced and pandemic fears dissipated by 2022, home prices rose swiftly and reached all-time highs.

This graph from the Federal Reserve Bank of St. Louis displays average sales prices from 1963 and the first quarter of 2022. (the most recent data available). locations that are marked as U.S. territory include light gray colored. The Great Recession coincided with the real estate market's biggest decline prior to the COVID-19 epidemic. We still don't know what the coronavirus outbreak will do to society in the long run.

Rental houses

If you invest in rental properties, you will become a landlord, so you should consider whether you'll be comfortable in that role. Finding tenants, maintaining the home, paying the mortgage, insurance, and property taxes will all fall under your purview. You will also be responsible for managing any problems that may emerge. Unless you hire a property manager to handle the details, being a landlord takes a lot of time and work. Depending on your situation, taking care of the property and the tenants may be a 24/7 job that isn't always pleasurable. However, you can reduce the likelihood of experiencing serious issues if you choose your renters and properties properly.

Rent is one way that landlords can generate income.

How much rent you can charge will depend on where the property is located. Nevertheless, determining the ideal rent can be difficult because if you charge too much, you risk losing tenants, and if you charge too little, you risk losing money. It's common practice to just collect the minimum amount of rent necessary to cover expenses up until the mortgage is paid off, after which the remainder is turned into profit.

Appreciation is the other primary source of income for landlords.

You might be able to sell your property for a profit (when the time is right) or take out a loan against the equity to pay for your next investment if the value of your property increases. There are no assurances, even if real estate does frequently increase in value.

This is especially true when the real estate market is experiencing high levels of volatility, most notably during the COVID-19 epidemic. The United States' median real estate prices increased by an astounding 38% between February 2020 and March 2022.

Many people have begun to wonder if prices are about to drop due to the extraordinary surge.

renovating homes

Like day traders are miles apart from buy-and-hold investors, real estate flippers are an entirely different breed from landlords who buy and rent out their properties. Houses are bought by flippers with the intention of holding them for a little period—typically no more than three to four months—and then quickly selling them for a profit.

There are two primary ways to flip a property:

Renovate and fix. Using this method, you buy a house that you think will increase in value after minor alterations and upgrades. The ideal scenario is to complete the project as soon as feasible and then sell it for a profit (including the renovations).

Keep and re-sell. In this instance, flipping operates differently. As an alternative to purchasing a home and making modifications to it, you buy in a market that is fast increasing, keep for a while, and then sell for a profit.

With any kind of flipping, there is a risk that you won't be able to sell the house at a price that will net you a profit. Because flippers often don't keep enough cash on hand to cover long-term mortgage payments on houses, this can be challenging. Flipping, however, could be a successful strategy to invest in real estate if done right.

REITs Real estate investment trusts (REITs) are created when a corporation (or trust) is established with the goal of employing investor capital to buy, manage, and resell properties that generate income. REITs can be purchased and sold on significant exchanges, just like stocks and exchange-traded funds (ETFs).

To qualify as a REIT, a corporation must pay out dividends to shareholders equal to 90% of its taxable income. In contrast to a regular firm, which would have to pay tax on its profits and limit the returns it can offer shareholders, REITs are able to avoid paying corporate income tax by doing this.

Similar to regular dividend-paying stocks, REITs are suitable for investors seeking reliable income, yet they also provide the potential for profit. Office buildings, mortgages, malls (about a quarter of all REITs specialize in these), and healthcare facilities are just a few of the diverse types of properties that REITs invest in. The high level of liquidity offered by REITs gives them an edge over other real estate investing techniques.

Real estate investment groups, sometimes known as REIGs, are like mini-mutual funds for rental properties. If you want to own a rental property but don't want the hassles of being a landlord, a real estate investment group may be the solution for you.

A company will buy or build a group of buildings, typically apartments, and then allow investors to buy those buildings straight from the company. A single investor may own self-contained residential units in one or more buildings. The company that manages the investment group, however, administers each property and takes care of upkeep, marketing, and tenant placement. In exchange for this management, the company receives a percentage of the monthly rent.

There are various types of investment groups.

In the standard arrangement, the investor is identified on the lease and all units split a portion of the rent to guard against irregular vacancies. This suggests that you will still receive enough to pay the mortgage even if your apartment is empty. The quality of an investment group is entirely dependent on the firm that offers it. Though theoretically a safe option to begin investing in real estate, some organizations might charge exorbitant fees similar to those that afflict the mutual fund industry. For any investment, research is crucial.

• Restricted partnerships for property
Real estate limited partnerships (RELPs) and real estate investment groups are comparable. It is a business set up to buy

and hold a number of properties, or possibly just one. The longevity of RELPs is constrained, though. A seasoned property management or real estate development firm serves as the general partner. Then, the real estate project is looking for outside investors to provide capital in exchange for a stake as limited partners. When the properties are eventually sold, ideally at a sizable profit, and the RELP is dissolved, that is when the real return is realized. The income produced by the properties of the RELP may be distributed to the partners on a regular basis.

Real Estate Mutual Funds

The primary goals of real estate mutual funds are REITs and real estate operating companies. With comparatively little capital, they enable the ability to get diverse exposure to real estate. They offer investors a far wider selection of assets than is possible by purchasing individual REITs, depending on their strategy and diversification goals. These funds are fairly liquid, much like REITs.

Another significant advantage is the research and analytical data that the fund makes available to regular investors. This could include details on recently purchased assets as well as management's evaluation of the viability and performance of specific real estate investments and as an asset class. Riskier investors have access to a family of real estate mutual funds where they can selectively overweight specific property types. or

Why Make a Real Estate Investment?

The risk-and-return profile of an investor's portfolio can be improved by real estate since it provides competitive risk-adjusted returns. The real estate market frequently displays modest volatility, particularly when compared to the markets for equities and bonds.

Real estate is even more alluring when compared to other traditional sources of income return. During times of low Treasury rates, this asset class is particularly appealing because it often trades at a yield premium to U.S. Treasuries.

Protection and diversification

Diversification is another opportunity in real estate investing. Due to its poor correlation with other significant asset classes—possibly even a negative one—real estate typically increases when equities decline. As a result, it can be concluded that including real estate in a portfolio will lower volatility and increase return on risk. The more direct the real estate investment, the stronger the hedge: Publicly traded securities with a lower degree of directness, such as REITs, will mirror the performance of the stock market as a whole.

Because it is supported by physical structures, direct real estate also involves less principal-agent conflict, or the degree to which the investor's interest is dependent on the integrity and competence of managers and borrowers. Even the more deceptive investment strategies offer some safety. REITs, for example, mandate that a minimum percentage of profits (90%) be paid out as dividends.

Given that REIT stocks are now part of the S&P 500, many analysts anticipate a closer relationship between the stock market and REITs.

Contingency Hedging

Because there is a link between rising real estate demand and GDP growth, real estate has the ability to act as an inflation hedge

(GDP). Because there is more demand for real estate when economies grow, rents rise along with capital values. Thus, by transmitting some inflationary pressure onto tenants and by incorporating some inflationary pressure, in the form of capital appreciation, real estate has a tendency to maintain the purchasing power of capital.

Leverage: The Power of It

With the exception of REITs, stock market investors do not have access to the tool of leverage that real estate investors enjoy. The phrase "leverage" refers to borrowing funds to finance a larger purchase than you are able to afford. You must pay the entire stock price at the time the buy order is submitted, barring purchases made on leverage. Even then, the proportion you can borrow is still much smaller than with real estate because of that wonderful financing mechanism, the mortgage.

Typical down payments for conventional mortgages are around 20%.

You might, however, be able to obtain a mortgage that requires only 5% down, depending on where you live. Therefore, merely investing a small portion of the overall value, you can own the entire property and the equity it contains. Of course, the amount of ownership you actually have in the home depends on the size of your mortgage, but you take control of it as soon as the paperwork is signed.

This increases the confidence of both landlords and real estate investors. They can obtain a second mortgage on their principal residences while putting down payments on two or three additional properties. They are in charge of these assets, regardless of whether they hold onto them until they have the chance to sell for a profit or rent them out so that tenants pay the mortgage.

How Can I Expand My Portfolio with Real Estate?

Regular investors can invest in REITs or funds that invest in REITs as alternatives to directly buying real estate. Investing in real estate or mortgages can be done through REITs, which are collective investments.

Why Is Real Estate Considered an Inflation Hedge?

Usually, property values rise along with inflation. This is because in order to keep up with inflation, costs connected with building new dwellings must rise. However, current property prices also go up with inflation. The rise in inflation makes your fixed monthly payments on a fixed-rate mortgage more reasonable. As a landlord, you can also increase the rent to account for inflation.

Why Do Interest Rates Affect Home Prices?

Loans are frequently needed to finance the purchase of real estate because of its size and cost. Rising interest rates thus raise the price of mortgage payments for new loans (or on existing adjustable-rate loans like ARMs). That may put off potential purchasers who must account for the expense of maintaining the property month to month.

the outcome
Real estate has the potential to enhance wealth and provide a reliable source of income. An ongoing drawback of real estate investing is its illiquidity, or the relative difficulty in converting one asset into another or from one financial source to another.
When compared to stock or bond transactions, which may be completed in a

matter of seconds, real estate deals might take weeks or even months to complete. Even with a broker's help, it can take weeks to find the right counterparty. Of course, REITs and real estate mutual funds provide greater liquidity and market pricing. However, they come with a higher risk than direct real estate investments because of their far closer connection to the overall stock market.

Just as with any investment, keep your expectations in check. Before making any decisions, make sure to complete your research and homework. Discrimination in mortgage lending is prohibited. If you feel that you have been the victim of discrimination due to your race, religion, sex, gender, marital status, use of public assistance, national origin, handicap, or age, there are legal steps you can take. One of these actions is submitting a report to the U.S. Department of Housing and Urban

Development (HUD) or the Consumer Financial Protection Bureau (CFPB) (HUD).

Contrary Investments Investing In Real Estate

REITs vs. landlords: Benefits And Drawbacks

Investors might purchase shares of real estate investment trusts or look for rental properties to buy and hold for exposure to the real estate market (REIT). Although owning a rental property provides you greater negotiating power and increases your chance of making sizable profits, it also comes with a long list of hassles, like collecting rent and taking care of maintenance issues. REITs provide a substantially simpler way to invest in real estate and receive consistent income through dividends, but they often have less upside potential and less control than rental properties.

Landlord Pros

There are several advantages to being a landlord. The greatest advantage might be leverage. individuals with excellent credit can put as little as 20% down and finance the remainder when purchasing rental property.

Therefore, the investor's financial investment is only $20,000 for a $100,000 home. If the property's value increases by 20% in the first year, which is not unheard of in a competitive real estate market, the investor will get a 100% return. A wise real estate investor creates enough rental income to pay the mortgage and yet make a profit, despite the fact that mortgage payments must be made on the amount borrowed. As a result, the investor benefits from both property growth and rent collections from tenants.

Landlord Cons

Being a landlord is significantly less passive than owning shares in a REIT. Many people who started making rental property investments quickly learned that keeping track of all of their properties was a full-time job in and of itself. Anyone considering making an investment in rental properties needs to be ready to put in a lot of time, or be willing to employ a professional property manager to handle the minutiae like renting out vacant apartments, collecting rent, and dealing with late renters.

Then there are all the expenses related to property ownership. Depending on how the lease agreement is written, a landlord may be financially responsible for anything from a leaky faucet to a broken refrigerator. An investor's profit may be quickly reduced as a result. Moreover, dealing with frantic late-night phone calls every time a tenant's toilet does not flush properly can impede quality of life.

REIT Pros

Purchasing REIT shares as opposed to rental properties is undoubtedly more convenient. REIT investing enables one to share in value increase and rental income without having to deal with the bother of actually buying, managing, and selling real estate. Another advantage of diversification. Building a broad portfolio of one's own rental properties requires a significant budget, a lot of work, and a lot of knowledge. With just one simple investment, the proper REIT offers done-for-you diversity. Additionally, even while purchasing rental properties may be profitable, doing so has a high risk, particularly if the real estate market declines. REIT shares, on the other hand, can be converted into cash in a single, five-minute phone call.

REIT Cons

REITs are not eligible for the leverage benefit of financing rental properties. The law mandates that a REIT distribute 90% of its profits to investors, leaving just 10% available for the company to grow by acquiring additional properties. As a result, REIT share prices rarely rise as quickly as, for instance, those of Silicon Valley tech companies. These companies rarely pay dividends and frequently devote every last penny of their earnings to growth and innovation.

Having control over your rental property is greater than buying REITs. An investor has the chance to see, touch, and smell a rental property before buying it. The investor might research the local rental market as well as the recent performance of comparable properties. You are purchasing REIT shares, you are handing over control. This can be ideal for investors not wanting to make such decisions, but those who prefer a hands-on approach might be better off as landlords.

How Do You Invest In Real Estate?

Real estate investing is the buying of real estate. To fully understand the phrase "real estate," we must first define it. The ground and the things that are attached to it are both considered real estate. Everything on this ground, be it a tree, a building, a fence, or anything else, is referred to as "real estate."

It is common to interchange the terms "land," "real estate," and "real property." However, there are extremely slight differences between each sentence. The term "land" refers to any natural surface or airspace that you would perceive to be a part of Mother Earth. Real estate consists of this ground as well as any durable buildings that people have erected, such a house. All of the incentives and opportunities in real estate associated with owning real estate.

Therefore, purchasing a piece of land and any alterations made by people is investing in real estate. Residential, commercial, and industrial real estate investing are the three most popular types of real estate investing.
Even though it may at first seem expensive, investing in real estate is one of the most tried-and-true ways to build wealth. We then discuss the potential financial benefits of real estate investing.

How Can Investing in Real Estate Be Successful?

There are many various ways to make money through real estate investing, which is a tried-and-true method. The two fundamental tactics are value growth and rental income.

Property values have increased over time due to value appreciation. Appreciation refers to this increase in value. Any professional would agree that location is the most crucial aspect to take into account when making an investment. Property values rise in direct proportion to how attractive a neighborhood is seen as being. Ever hear the adage, "Buy the house in the best neighborhood that looks the worst?" There is some truth to this. Buying a house you can renovate in a desired neighborhood is preferable to buying a decent house in an undesirable one. You might think about investing in a developing region.

For rental income, some real estate investors will only count on value growth. They might buy a vacation home or settle on the property, for example. But a lot of real estate investors prefer to increase their wealth through rental income. By renting out the property, you are generating a monthly income in addition to the long-term growth of the asset. Depending on how much work you want to put into it, some landlords who hire a property manager may be able to classify this income as passive.

In an ideal world, your renters would pay off your mortgage and make you a little bit of money. (It will produce a pure profit once the mortgage is paid off.) However, be careful to include maintenance and repairs in your budget.

Tips For Beginners On Real Estate Investing

If you've never invested in real estate before, it can be intimidating to get started. It may take several years before an investor feels safe and confident investing in real estate.

Because of this, it makes sense to use beginner-friendly investment strategies. Even though they are suitable for investors with little to no experience, they can nevertheless be extremely rewarding when handled properly.

It's a great idea to start in a market that welcomes new investors before moving on to more challenging ventures. Instead of committing to a project, investors can learn about their local market, build a network, and gain knowledge about how to raise money by starting with an achievable proposal they might not be able to handle. Then, investors might later switch to different tactics using their knowledge and earnings.

To get you started, consider these real estate investment tactics for newbies:

Wholesaling: Using this strategy, investors can operate as a middleman between buyers and sellers. A property that is below market value will be found by wholesalers, who will then secure it and assign the contract to an end user. Prehabbing is the process of making a few minor cosmetic upgrades to a home in order to get it ready for selling. The house is typically sold to an investor who would completely refurbish it after that.

Companies that own and manage properties with an income potential are known as real estate investment trusts (REITs). Then, without really owning any real estate, investors can benefit from the profitability of real estate by purchasing shares in a REIT.

Online real estate platforms: These enable developers and investors to collaborate more easily. The investors contribute to the funding of real estate developments in exchange for consistent, monthly or quarterly interest-bearing payments.

If you're ready to become a landlord, purchasing rental properties is a great way to ensure a steady revenue stream. If you do not want to be a landlord, you can work with property management. Property syndication Real estate syndication is a crowdfunding variant that stresses cooperation. Investors pool their resources and talents to buy vast properties and divide the profits.

House flipping is one of the most popular ways to start a career in real estate. The process of acquiring a home, making renovations, and then selling it for profit is known in real estate as flipping.

Real Estate Investment Groups (REIG):

A real estate investment group is a business that carries out most of its operations in real estate. It pools money from several investors to invest in commercial or multi-unit properties.

1. Real estate wholesale

One of the simplest ways to get started in real estate is through wholesaling. Buying a property for less than market value and appointing a final consumer to assume the contract is this unique strategy. Wholesalers never actually own the property; instead, they are compensated by adding a fee to the final contract.

A strong buyer list is necessary for profitable wholesaling. In essence, this is a list of prospective investors looking for their next deal. Wholesalers commonly run lead generating campaigns. to find potential customers. In order to do this, they must first establish a list of potential investors and market their company, frequently via emails, social media, or direct mail. You will require the names, contact details, type of funding, and buying criteria of investors in order to establish a buyers list.

By doing this, you can be sure that you are aware of the kinds of deals they are looking for and how to contact them after you have found the appropriate house. Wholesaling is a great real estate investment strategy for beginning investors because it doesn't cost much money to get started. Investors won't be buying properties, but they might require money for good faith payments or successful marketing. Investors can also build a strong network and gain a deep grasp of the local sector by investing in wholesale business.

2. Real Estate Prehab

A great way to start investing in real estate is through prehab. Prehab projects only call for minor modifications in contrast to rehab projects, which demand for money for significant adjustments. Investors will typically make little improvements to a property in order to attract more investors. Prehabbing entails making small, incremental improvements to a property as opposed to major ones. Prehab projects include the following:

+Cleaning: Making the time to give a property a complete cleaning, including removing any trash and debris, will greatly improve its appeal.

+Painting: For amateurs, painting is a practical way to improve a building's appearance.

+Landscaping: I promise that if you can't make people appreciate the building's exterior, they won't want to take the time to walk inside. Despite being quite inexpensive, curb appeal has a significant effect on real estate.

Not all homes will lend themselves well to a prehab, therefore investors thinking about using this strategy should be aware of that. Search for buildings with solid structural integrity that only require "basic" cleaning; avoid homes that might require pricey repairs straight away. Location is important while looking for pre-rehab homes, another important consideration. Do some market research to find the hotspots and emerging areas.

Understanding the attractiveness of prehabbing should be straightforward after you discover how to invest in real estate. In comparison to other investment strategies, it not only entails less risk and work but will also produce results quickly. Remember that selling the sizzle, not the steak, is the main focus of prehab.

3. Investing in REITs Real estate investment trusts (REITs) are a great place to start for those who are new to the real estate market. Equity The most common kind, REITs, are simply companies that possess real estate with the ability to generate revenue. Investors purchase shares in these companies, and as a result, they regularly get dividend payments. REITs are advantageous since they can generate reliable passive income.

While investing in REITs may be compared to stock investing, The Motley Fool points out that REITs usually offer dividends that are above average. Start by learning more about publicly traded REITs and evaluating their performance records. Analyze the company's current dividends, predicted growth, and cash flow (FFO). An excellent alternative for selecting a REIT to invest in is to speak with a financial counselor.

Despite the fact that plenty of investors use REITs to diversify their present assets, they are still a wonderful way to enter the real estate industry. Since they provide those who might not be ready or able to buy real estate the chance to profit from it, REITs are often an excellent alternative for beginning investors. Despite the fact that there are a number of factors that can influence the performance of REITs, this investment option is known for offering solid returns with relatively low risk.

4. Real estate websites
Online marketplaces for real estate, commonly referred to as real estate crowdfunding marketplaces, help to connect borrowers and investors. Investors can decide to lend money or put up stock to finance a business or a project when a developer offers a contract or a project that needs funding. Investors can profit from real estate investing as a result without

having to worry about ownership or labor, creating a win-win situation.

The project-related funding needed by developers is accessible. Keep in mind that financing real estate deals can be just as risky and speculative as directly investing in real estate. Before making a choice, research the matter thoroughly. Investors may choose to fund either monthly or quarterly payments that they receive, and they have the option of funding either individual projects or a portfolio of projects. It's also a terrific method to geographically diversify your real estate investments. The funds may be illiquid and subject to lockup periods when using a real estate platform, and investors must pay platform membership fees.

5. Purchasing real estate to rent out

Are you ready to be a property owner? Buying rental properties could be a great way to ensure a reliable monthly income. If you feel you can handle the requirements of being a landlord, you will surely enjoy having a consistent source of income.

If you buy a rental property at the right moment and in the right market, you could even be able to use the rent you earn to pay your mortgage, maintenance fees, and repair fees. (Better yet, you might even increase your earnings!) Owners of rental properties have the option of making this income source active or passive. A property manager can be hired by landlords who would rather not "landlord" at all. Some landlords decide to outsource only the upkeep and repairs, while others may decide to handle everything themselves in order to save expenses and increase profits.

When making investments in rental properties, you might also consider "home hacking". This suggests that you'll just occupy one room in the building while renting out the others. You could also buy a house with numerous flats and live in one of them. Even if you want to make money from the house by renting it out, this could make it easier for you to get a mortgage.

Property Syndication, No. 6
Real estate syndication is the association of real estate investors for the purpose of locating and acquiring properties. A sponsor and other investors often split the responsibilities.

The sponsor is responsible for locating potential investors and securing the contract. Additionally, they could be in charge of supervising the property. Sponsors often donate their expertise and effort rather than money to the investment.

Investors in a syndication arrangement fund the purchase as well as any additional costs needed to renovate or maintain the property. Investors have a more passive role and are compensated over time through monthly or quarterly returns. The syndication portion of the deal is completed after the exit plan is a success. For instance, once the property has been renovated and sold. Sponsors will receive a set amount in exchange for their participation in the transaction.

7. Reselling homes

You probably already have a basic understanding of what house flipping entails if HGTV was one of the inspirations behind your decision to begin investing in real estate. In essence, you locate a home that is being offered below market value. Typically, it needs some remodeling and repair. The property is then sold for a profit after renovations have been made.

When conducting their financial research, investors who are interested in flipping houses should be aware of the hazards and exercise extreme caution. Many things may go wrong. First of all, if you go above your renovation budget, you run the risk of losing money. You run the risk of not being able to sell the house if the pricing or market conditions are unfavorable. If you've never flipped a house before, you might want to think about doing it with a partner who has the necessary expertise.

8. Institutions that invest in real estate (REIG)

A real estate investment group is a business that focuses on real estate investments (REIG). In order to buy apartment complexes and commercial real estate, it aggregates investor capital. They might even choose to buy houses, refurbish them, and then resell them.

Real Estate Investment Groups (REIGs) differ slightly from Real Estate Investment Trusts (REITs) in the way their operations are structured. They might change the way they invest and employ a variety of strategies to diversify their cash flows. REIGs are widely used by investors who want to profit from the real estate market without having to perform property management responsibilities.

INVESTING IN PROPERTY FOR NEWCOMERS

Benefits of Investing in Real Estate
The benefits of real estate investing are numerous, ranging from better leverage to long-term stability. One of the perks of real estate investing that investors cite most frequently is the tax advantages. Real estate can be a great instrument for lowering your tax obligations because of the wide range of possible deductions. These comprise the depreciation and business write-offs, deduction, and a pass-through deduction for LLC owners.

When considering leverage, real estate is a great way to grow equity in an investment. Property values often rise over time, enabling your equity to rise apart from loan payments. This might be quite beneficial if you need money to finance the purchase of a new home or another type of investment because you can use your current equity as leverage when looking for new financing.

Real estate can significantly diversify an investing portfolio. In contrast to equities, which are regarded to be risky, real estate is a stable investment type throughout time. Similar to that, it frequently does well in market shocks (where stocks may be more susceptible to dramatic pricing changes). Real estate can be used by investors to hedge against inflation. Since the demand for real estate frequently rises when the economy expands, owners can profit from higher appreciation, increased rental demand, and more.

Another benefit of real estate is its long-term stability, which can be seen by looking at its historical performance over time. Additionally, this asset class can provide investors with a source of passive income, especially for landlords who engage with property managers and hold rental properties. There are many different real estate investing strategies to pick from, giving the niche a lot of freedom.

The Top 10 Characteristics of Succeeding Real Estate Investors

As a beginning real estate investor, it might be easy to begin doubting yourself and your potential for success. But no success tale ever has a perfect beginning. According to real estate billionaire Warren Buffett, temperament, not intelligence, is the most important quality in an investor. You can always recreate yourself, by drawing from your past mistakes. You can start modeling some of the following characteristics of successful real estate investors right now:

- Passionate
- Self-disciplined
- Driven
- Imaginative
- Bold
- Principled
- Flexible
- Economical
- Team-oriented
- Personable

The Importance of Networking

As many investing clubs and networking gatherings as possible should be attended by prospective investors. It may initially appear disturbing, but anyone who wants to enter the industry will need to make some contacts. After your initial meetings, research internet networking tips and look for a mentor. By chatting with real estate experts, you can obtain detailed guidance on how to close agreements and solve challenges. At neighborhood networking events, you might even hear information that is exclusive to your market.

In addition to being a great place to learn, networking events are also a great method to establish contacts. Your interactions with others will eventually affect how you approach investments and find your real estate specialization when it comes to real estate investing for beginners. Once you start closing a business, having the appropriate staff to rely on will be essential.

Another thing to keep in mind when networking is to always use caution when corresponding with other investors. Take in as much knowledge as you can, but make sure to research everything you discover. Just because something didn't work for someone else doesn't mean it will necessarily not work for you in the same market or area.

Make a real estate business plan.
The creation of a business plan is a great place for a beginner investor to begin investing. By doing this, you'll be able to figure out your "why". You might want to increase your family's financial situation or put money aside for retirement, for instance. The best advice I can give you if you're new to real estate investing is to make sure you're honest about your goals, says Independent Property Group owner Matthew Peden.

Being a beginner investor, you must be truthful about whether or not you intend to live in the property you own or sell it for a profit. Even though you now have more resources than you did when you first started, make sure the complexity of this type of investment is still within your capacity.

Whatever your motivation, it would be quite beneficial to picture it before starting. The next step in developing a business plan is to put your specific business goals in writing. It may sound unusual at first, but a real estate business plan acts as a roadmap for investors. You'll be able to identify and describe your objectives while also planning concrete next measures.

With the proper preparation, a real estate business plan can be a useful teaching tool for those who are new to real estate investing. Take a look at Beginner's Guide To Real Estate. If you are honest about wanting to start a real estate firm, it is essential to learn everything you can about it. The many books, blogs, and magazines on investing are a great place to start.

Despite the wealth of options available, first attempt to pace yourself. Instead, invest just 15 minutes each day in learning something new by picking up a few investing books or subscribing to a real estate newsletter. Being lifelong learners is a quality that all successful real estate investors possess. Throughout your life, adopting a mindset of lifelong learning will be a beneficial career as an investor. For some suggestions to get you started, look over our collection of real estate investing books.

Start now
Finally, the best way to learn the real estate industry is through hands-on experience. If you aren't quite ready to go it alone, consider seeing a local real estate specialist work on your next deal. You might need to help out with a few errands to make their time worthwhile, but after networking with

other professionals, you shouldn't have any issue finding a link to shadow while you learn the skills.

Knowing how to make offers and bargain with actual sellers will be of enormous use as you launch your own real estate business. If you tour properties with other professionals, you'll also gain a better understanding of what to look for when you're ready to start buying. For the long haul, first-hand experience will be beneficial, particularly for newcomers in real estate investing.

Mistakes To Avoid When Investing In Real Estate

There are many methods to get started in real estate investing. However, as you begin your route, you should refrain from performing a few things in order to achieve. Take some time to learn from other people's mistakes and make a list of instances that you might encounter in the course of your work. You can learn a lot from your coach and other contacts. Here are some additional typical errors to avoid while investing in real estate:

+Following the herd: When first starting out, it may be tempting to do so. One of the worst real estate investing strategies for novices is to rely on speculation and cross your fingers that a property will appreciate in value. Buying a home at market value offers very few benefits. Real estate investors specialize in locating excellent bargains or buying distressed homes for significantly less than market value.

Feeling something You quickly form an emotional relationship to one of the first potential offers you come across. But it's important to keep your composure and carry yourself with professionalism. Regardless of how alluring an offer initially seems, one should always.

+Lack of multiple exit strategies: Investors should be prepared for the possibility that projects won't proceed as planned, which is certain to happen periodically. Because of this, seasoned investors have various fallback options. In the event a house flip fails, have a backup strategy in place, such as wholesaling or a buy-and-hold strategy.

+Going it alone: Despite what some may believe, investing in real estate is not something that should be undertaken alone. Some could even claim that being a "people person" is essential for success in the real estate investing industry. Investors who want to succeed must have a trustworthy network of professionals they can consult when they need assistance finding their next venture, forming a partnership, or seeking advice.

Reading List For Real Estate Beginners

If you want to diversify your current reading list, there are several books regarding real estate investing. You may learn about the basics of investing, business lingo, crucial strategies, and more from these publications. Here is a selection of a few books to get you started:

Investing in Real Estate with No (and Low) Money Down by Brandon Turner The purpose of this book is to get you thinking like an investor. Turner's ideas can help readers by teaching them how to make the most of their financial circumstances and reach agreements utilizing other people's money.

Building Wealth One House at a Time by John Schaub: This book is methodology-focused. If you want to learn how to buy properties, generate money, and replicate the results, this book is fantastic. Due to his more than 30 years of real estate investing experience, Schaub's book is a great place for beginners to start.

The E-Myth by Michael Gerber Investor in real estate This is the cornerstone of real estate investing. The E-Myth helps novice investors to view investment from a different angle. To get you started, the book offers an overview of sound business principles and frameworks for investing.

The Real Estate Rehab Investing Bible by Paul Esajian: A Proven-Profit Method for Finding, Financing, Fixing, and Flipping Homes Without Picking Up a Brush If house flipping is the strategy you are most interested in, think about starting here. Esajian offers advice on how to finance each purchase and outlines the best methods for sliding residences that are profitable. The essential techniques for examining offers described in the book will be useful to investors of all levels of experience.

The Fastest, Simplest Way to Start Investing in Real Estate: The Real Estate Wholesaling Bible by Than Merrill Sometimes wholesale is thought to be the best strategy for novice real estate investors. A book teaches how to grow this doable side venture for newbies into a full-fledged real estate enterprise. Merrill's recommendations include tips on how to find funding for beginners and how to break into tough markets.

Real Estate Terminology Newcomers Need to Know

When learning how to invest in real estate, one of the first things you'll notice is the abundance of acronyms and industry-specific lingo. In order to connect with your new colleagues in the industry, it is important to comprehend at least the fundamentals of real estate jargon, even though there are many of them.

Take note of the following terms to get you started:

Capitalization Rate: The capitalization rate, sometimes known as the "cap rate," is a formula used to estimate the value of an investment agreement. The cap rate, which is calculated as a percentage, is always based on the property's current market value.

In both personal and business finance, the word "cash flow" is used to describe the inflows and outflows of cash. The total rental income the property earns less all expenses, for example, is the monthly cash flow that a landlord usually calculates. Investors will search for homes that have a healthy cash flow each month.

The calculation of cash flows and net operating income (NOI), also referred to as

NOI, work hand in hand. Your net operating profit is the amount that remains after deducting all monthly expenses from monthly rental income. Simply described, this is the area of the business that produces profits.

REITs are companies that typically hold and manage portfolios of assets that bring in money from real estate. Particular markets, such as the residential or commercial ones, may be the emphasis of some REITs. For investors who want to take a more passive approach to real estate investing, REITs may be fantastic options.

REO properties are ones that lenders, typically banks, have reclaimed and are now the owners of. After a foreclosure, a lender would often remove liens and fees from a property so that it can be sold more quickly. REO homes are a great option for real estate investors looking to purchase properties for less than market value. Return On

Investment (ROI): The preferred statistic for comparing the effectiveness of an investment agreement is the return on investment (ROI). The relationship between net profit and capital used for the investment determines ROI. The gains are better when the ratio is larger.

Are Investing in Real Estate a Good Idea?
The decision to invest in real estate is quite personal. Although your preferred investing strategy may be risky, it also has the potential to generate substantial profits. Real estate investing has been demonstrated to yield reliable, long-term profitability. Furthermore, the real estate market's performance isn't always correlated with the stock market, making it a great method to diversify your investments.

Real estate is another incredibly sensible investment. For instance, you might occupy it while performing a lucrative makeover. Additionally, you may invest in a wonderful vacation rental that not only pays for itself but also occasionally allows for your personal usage. Recognize that if you want to invest in real estate, you might not always see a quick return. Although it requires a significant financial investment, the long-term benefits can be enormous.

Summary

Real estate has demonstrated time and time again to be a tremendously rewarding financial vehicle. But one of the largest obstacles to entrance is the complexity of real estate investing. The good news is that anyone can study real estate investing; all it needs is a little time spent on self-education. We made a specific beginner's guide for this reason. Whatever your starting point, there is no reason to bar access to real estate. Numerous investing strategies can be used to enter the lucrative real estate industry. Spend some time researching real estate investment for beginners to find the approach that works best for you.

CHAPTER FOUR

What Sets Limited Liability Companies Apart From Corporations?

Which entity will be most favorable to the business is the main worry while researching the legal differences between a corporation and a limited liability company (LLC). This is a challenging subject that will depend on your business plan as well as a variety of other elements, such as your need for international investments, asset protection, and tax duties.

Differences between an LLC and a corporation

Despite the fact that the title "limited liability company" does not contain the word "corporation," it is crucial to be aware that creating an LLC has many parallels to creating a corporation. However, an LLC is a hybrid legal form that combines characteristics of a corporation and a sole proprietorship or partnership (depending on the number of business owners).

In contrast to corporations, an LLC is distinct in that its members are also its owners. As a result, the LLC is practically free to distribute ownership shares among members without regard to any member's specific financial contributions to the LLC. A corporation, as opposed to an LLC, is owned by stockholders, making it a legal entity that is entirely and totally distinct from its owners.

Although this jargon may appear confusing at first glance, an LLC is actually protected from liability in a way that is comparable to how a corporation is. The expression "limited liability" is valid at this stage. However, because the LLC is taxed in a manner similar to that of an unincorporated business, business and income losses can be distributed to the owners for inclusion on their individual tax returns.

A corporation's profit is taxed through a "corporate tax," and after shareholders receive dividends, they are then subject to individual income tax. In contrast, an LLC's business and income losses are distributed directly to the owners. In order to demystify these admittedly complex topics, it would be beneficial to divide them into subsections that detail the different and important differences between these company structures.

The Crucial Difference Between a Tax Entity and a Legal Entity

In the event of a legal dispute, a company's legal categorization identifies how the government, clients and suppliers, and the legal system will see it. Tax categorization, on the other hand, solely and only pertains to how the Internal Revenue Service (IRS) and state tax authorities see the corporation. A corporation will thereafter be designated as a legal entity and receive the tax entity classification (either an S corp or C corp designation). In contrast, an LLC gets to pick its tax status. An LLC can choose the tax structure that will benefit its members the most thanks to this kind of flexibility, but this does not always imply that an LLC is the best option.

Corporations and LLCs and their Tax Effects

Double taxation appears to be one of the main disadvantages of a company. As was hinted at in the first section on the differences between an LLC and a corporation, a company may be taxed ordinarily as a C corporation. In the case of C corporations, corporate taxes must be paid by the business itself. The gains may subsequently be distributed as dividends to shareholders, who will then be responsible for paying personal income tax on these dividend distributions. For a number of reasons, this can be disadvantageous, which is why so-called S corporations are frequently selected.

Unlike C businesses, S firms are not subject to corporate income tax. In these businesses, all corporate profits are given to the shareholders, who are then in charge of paying personal income tax on the money. It is commonly known that pass-through taxes is a concept from which an LLC may also gain.

Even though this form of corporate structure has many advantages, a business may not be eligible to be a S corp if it meets the following requirements:

The corporation has more than 100 shareholders, there are foreign investors, or more than one class of shares is held by shareholders.

Once more, there are a variety of alternatives and degrees of flexibility when it comes to the tax implications of an LLC.

Because single-member LLCs are regarded as sole proprietorships whereas multi-member LLCs are regarded as partnerships, all LLC earnings and expenses are reported on members' individual income tax returns. Given that the members have already paid tax on their share of the earnings, the LLC might choose to be taxed as an S corporation or C corporation.

Why would an LLC favor C corp taxation? There are some really great reasons. Consider the possibility that the LLC wants to collaborate with foreign investors. Instead of the S corp ban on foreign shareholders, it would make more sense to incorporate as a C corp and accept the "double taxation" impact.

Instead, consider business owners who are also employed by the organization. As an alternative, imagine proprietors who are also employed by the company. To benefit from the self-employment tax benefits provided by S corporations in such a situation, it is customarily advisable to formally incorporate as a S company rather than an LLC.

When choosing whether to use an LLC operating agreement to form an LLC or a corporation, these are the kinds of legal considerations that must be made. Which Business Provides the Best Asset Protection? Although tax repercussions are typically the primary concern for the majority of firms, there are many other aspects that demand careful consideration. One such situation is asset protection.

According to state law, LLC assets may be shielded from "charging orders," such that in the event of a lawsuit against a business owner, the only assets that may be attached are the dividends from the LLC. Although the majority of states demand that an LLC have at least two owners, some even treat single-member LLCs as sole proprietorships under this protection.

The fact that some states, like California and New York, have the authority to compel the sale of a company's assets, however, should be highlighted means that this protection is not federally enforceable. C and S corporations provide an alternative that clearly separates business ownership and management. This suggests that any obligations the business incurs will be protected against by personal responsibility defense for the company.

Individual shareholders will not escape responsibility for financial contributions and investments made to the company even though their personal assets are often protected. The same protection is often provided to corporate managers as well. Let's assume, however, that you are to blame for the accident for which you are being sued. A crucial limitation to remember is that, in the event that you possess shares in the business, a judgment creditor may be able to reach those shares in the great majority of states.

International Investing

An LLC is often the best choice of entity when foreign investments will have a significant impact on the business, though this is not always the case. Foreign investors will often be more drawn to an LLC corporate form because of the flexibility, opportunity for pass-through taxation, and ability to protect assets as discussed above.

Also keep in mind that a S company is the only legal business structure allowed in the US that excludes foreign investors. As a result, any company seeking foreign investment must automatically rule out the S corporation from consideration.

C corporations, however, provide significant benefits to overseas owners, particularly in nations like Canada that have similar tax structures. Nevertheless, an LLC can elect to be treated as a C corporation, offering the same benefits of a C corporation in addition to the generally easier tax management that an LLC offers.

REAL ESTATE INVESTMENT STRATEGY

A fantastic way to diversify your financial portfolio is through real estate investing.

Real estate has no connection to the stock market and home prices are much less unpredictable than those of securities. Property owners can also take advantage of numerous tax breaks, which boosts their investment's return. Finally, diversifying an investor's rental property portfolio across several regions makes them more resilient and able to withstand various economic crises.

Just as there are many different kinds of real estate assets, there are several kinds of real estate investing (commercial real estate, single-family rental property, apartment complexes, real estate wholesaling, real estate debt, and others).

Which strategy is appropriate for a particular investor will depend on their degree of risk tolerance, the amount of control they want over the asset, whether they are inexperienced or seasoned real estate investors, how much cash they have available for a down payment, and how much cash flow they require.

Here are some strategies for investing in real estate.

1. Invest in rental properties for one household (SFRs).
Due to a combination of fixed-rate mortgages, gradual price growth, and tax incentives that encourage home purchases, residential real estate is one of the most effective engines for fostering intergenerational prosperity in the United States. Rental property is one of the most promising real estate investments.

After the housing catastrophe of 2008, single family homes were widely acknowledged as a highly investable asset. Since then, they have grown into the largest asset class in real estate, with a value of $4.6 trillion. The SFR and build-to-rent sectors will receive over $45 billion in institutional finance in 2021, according to John Burns Real Estate Consulting.

Although there have been ups and downs in particular markets, as this chart from the Federal Reserve of St. Louis demonstrates, overall house values have improved.

Investors may employ leverage by borrowing from banks to finance assets that offer rental income (cash-on-cash) as well as capital growth over time. If not entirely, the monthly rental payment goes toward paying off the mortgage, so the investor builds equity.

Real estate also guards against inflation, which over time diminishes the value of fixed mortgage payments. Rental property is an essential part of a diversified investment portfolio because of its low correlation to the stock market.

2. Housebreaking

The down payments on investment mortgages may be too expensive for some would-be investors. Through "house-hacking," buyers could hasten the process of building equity in rental properties. Simply said, house hacking is when an investor buys a house to live in and rents out a portion of it. They can reduce their mortgage payments and, in certain situations, even make a profit with the rental revenue.

The so-called passive income is available for use in any way the home hacker sees fit, including paying off the mortgage, making a significant purchase, or even saving for a second property to expand their portfolio. The investor has access to residential mortgages, which have much lower down payments and interest rates than investment mortgages, which is one of the key advantages of home hacking.

3. Real estate flipping

Flipping entails renovating a home and then selling it quickly. Success in flipping is determined by the profit the seller makes over the purchase price and how quickly the property is sold because the flipper continues to make mortgage payments until the house is sold. Flippers search for bargains in purchases, make enough modifications to significantly increase the price, then sell the homes rapidly. If the flipper can make significant renovations while keeping expenditures in check, a distressed property can be the most enticing.

Successful flippers have a system in place that includes simple access to inexpensive supplies, a team that can perform work of a high grade for a fair price, and a real estate agent who can sell a house quickly. The disadvantage of flipping a home is that the seller will pay more capital gains taxes as a result than if the home had been owned for at least two years.

4. The internal reversal
As part of a live-in flip, a fixer-upper can be occupied while being upgraded and afterwards sold for a significant, tax-free profit. The live-in flipper loses money every month they own the property even though they use it while it is being rebuilt. Live-in flips can be very profitable if they can discover a home below market value or one where they can make modifications that will boost its worth because they can use owner-occupied financing to live in a home they are treating as an investment.

If the investor is qualified for low-interest loans like Veterans Administration loans, the live-in flip can be a powerful financial strategy. The U.S. tax system allows investors to sell a home and get gains of up to $500,000 for a couple or $250,000 for an individual without paying taxes. The investor must have owned and lived in the property for at least two of the five years prior to the sale in order to qualify for the Section 121 Exclusion.

Some investors utilize the proceeds from a live-in flip to purchase a nicer home in an effort to increase their wealth, pay off debt, or diversify their holdings. What is the live-in flip's disadvantage? The investor must change their location every few years while living on a construction site. And there's always a chance that the house has more significant issues. Another possibility is that an investor will have to leave while a live-in flip is in progress. If the following factors led to the move, you can be eligible for a partial Section 121 exclusion:

changing jobs, Health variations, a military presence, and unforeseen circumstances. If an investor is forced to act quickly, they should consult a tax professional.

5. Real estate wholesale
Real estate wholesaling comprises either charging a fee for the service or keeping the difference between what the seller receives and what the buyer pays in order to act as a middleman between a house buyer and a home seller. This typically involves "driving for dollars," or scouting for properties in neighborhoods that the investor thinks have the potential to be successful. Investors may also keep a look out for For Sale By Owner (FSBO) signs in addition to employing the Multiple Listing Service (MLS) and direct mail marketing.

6.Trusts that make real estate investments (REITs)
Real estate investors can invest without actually owning any real estate by using

REITs, or real estate investment trusts, which function as mutual funds. Investors purchase REIT shares in a manner akin to purchasing stock or mutual fund shares, and the trust pays dividends to its stockholders.

Congress established REITs in 1960 to enable people to invest in large-scale, income-producing real estate. REITs are entitled to deduct all dividend payments from their taxable corporate income. Since they transfer at least 100% of their taxable profits to shareholders, most REITs do not pay corporate tax, according to the Office of Investor Education and Advocacy of the Securities and Exchange Commission. In general, REITs are regarded as wise investments. The 40-year compounded annual return on REITs, as measured by the FTSE NAREIT Equity REIT Index, is 9.44 percent.

7. Real estate investment organizations (REIGs)

Real estate investment groups (REIGs), which are private investor organizations, pool their resources and knowledge to make real estate investments using a range of strategies. A real estate investment group does not have a board of directors that is subject to strict restrictions, in contrast to a REIT. For instance, REITs must have 100 investors by the end of their first year and five or fewer shareholders representing at least 50% of the REIT.

Contrarily, real estate investment groups are governed by private agreements as opposed to governmental regulations. The REIGs' organizational frameworks, membership costs, and degrees of participation are all adaptable. Investors that desire a stake in real estate should consider joining a real estate investment group.

8. Purchasing tax liens on real estate
One way to indirectly invest in real estate tax liens is to buy tax lien certificates. The

municipality where the residence is located will file a legal claim on the property known as a tax lien when an owner doesn't pay property taxes. It acts as a formal claim for the outstanding debt against the property. These are different from mortgage liens, which provide a lender the legal right to a property until the borrower repays the amount.

The certificate that is produced contains information about the amount owed, the interest rate that will be paid to the lien owner, and the date that the municipality put the tax lien on the property. The certificates are then offered for sale at an auction to investors; at the moment, 28 states permit the sale of these certificates. According to the National Tax Lien Association, property taxes go unpaid by over $21 billion each year, making it a substantial sector for investment.

When a bidder wins the auction, they pay the delinquent taxes, gain the right to either foreclose on the property or get their money back when the homeowner pays the unpaid taxes, depending on which option they choose. A predetermined amount of time is given to the homeowner to complete the payment or risk foreclosure.

9. Purchase, upgrade, lease, remortgage, and repeat

BRRR is a popular long-term real estate investing technique (Buy, Rehab, Rent, Refinance, Repeat).

The strategy entails getting a house, preferably for less than market value, renovating it, renting it out to pay the mortgage, getting a cash-out refinance, and then utilizing the profit to start the process all over again. This method is more suitable for seasoned investors than newbies, in part because it involves discovering incredible deals on homes that some renovate but are still a wise investment.

It is essential to comprehend the costs of the modifications that will make the rental property desirable to residents as well as how long they will take because the investor will be paying the mortgage while the work is being done. It's important to improve the property's curb appeal because kitchen and bathroom upgrades are typically the most profitable ones.

The next step is to find dependable tenants to rent the property to until the investor can refinance at a rate that at least covers the mortgage payments. Banks often require "seasoning" time prior to refinancing, and a cash-out refinance requires a specific level of equity. Lenders hardly ever refinance abandoned properties, thus the investor will also want a high credit score, such as 620 or above.

By finding another contract, the investor continues the process.

Even while it has the potential to be profitable, it is not a passive investing strategy. Given that it would be difficult to get a conventional mortgage on a distressed property, the investor might need to have access to a network of lenders or the ability to get a home equity line of credit (HELOC).

10. Increasing rent-related debt
Using this technique, you can pay off the debt on many rental properties and take ownership of them completely. According to financial expert Dave Ramsey, it may be used for both real estate investing and personal debt repayment.
The plan consists of:

acquiring several rental properties with low-interest loans, paying off the rental property with the lowest debt first with all available finances, and continuing the procedure, focusing on the lowest amount loan, until all are paid off. combining all rental income and savings from a job.

It's important to make the maximum monthly mortgage payment on the rental property with the lowest amount possible by using all of the available resources, such as day job savings and all rental revenue. The investor will continue to make the same amount of money when that is paid off, but there will be one less mortgage to settle. The reason the snowball effect happens is because the investor has more money after paying down one mortgage.

The strategy calls for locating high-quality rental properties with affordable mortgage interest rates and upholding a strict spending plan for the years required to carry out the plan. This method's advantages are plainly discernible and easily quantifiable, which has a substantial psychological advantage. Another advantage is that it is flexible, allowing the investor to delay the greater payments and stick to the minimum payments for however long is necessary if they have a minor financial setback.

11. BURL: rent, buy luxury items.

Utility costs are a crucial aspect of BURL. The owner loses money if a home's rental value exceeds the mortgage payment. They might be better off living in the smaller house and renting out the larger one if they possess a pretty luxurious home but could live happily in the latter. Rents typically increase along with inflation, so if the owner has owned the property for a considerable amount of time, it's probable that inflation has increased the potential rental income.

www.ingramcontent.com/pod-product-compliance
Lightning Source LLC
Chambersburg PA
CBHW070241220526
45465CB00004B/1478